LEEDS

Termini *by* Bob Pixton & John Hooper

Acknowledgements

This album was inspired by Peter Sunderland of Keighley whose photographs feature greatly throughout. Peter's kindness and generosity in allowing the authors to use, carte blanche, whatever illustrations took our fancy was refreshing indeed. By our third visit Peter must have wondered what he had let himself in for as we 'grilled' him about this view and that photograph, lineside pass's, this train, that train. Who, what, where and when? We hope that in the end he found the somewhat elongated exercise worth it. Although we must have tried his patience at times, he did not indicate any irritation and continued in good humour and still offered superb hospitality. Thank you Peter.

Likewise, David Laycock, an ex-Railwayman who spent much of his career at Leeds, imparted so much useful and valuable information about those often unreported aspects of railway history that would otherwise be lost.

Thanks also to David Beilby whose extensive knowledge of railways, and Leeds in particular, enabled some of the more obscure facts to surface in our captions.

We would also like to thank the following people and organisations for supplying information and photographs during the preparation of the album: The Rev. David Benson, Kenneth Fields, Roger Griffiths, Bernard Harding, Peter Kirton, Gavin Morrison, Mick Nicholson, Paul Smith, Neville Stead, Mrs Annie Yeadon. Fastline Photographic, the staff of the Public Record Office, Kew.

CHALLENGER U.K.

An aerial view of the Leeds termini in 1959. Looking in a north-westerly direction, the River Aire comes from the left alongside the old Wellington part of City station, before flowing south underneath the combined City North and South stations after which it curves east again at a point where it is joined by the Leeds & Liverpool canal. Running from top left to bottom right is City station where at the west end can be seen the former MR carriage repair shop on the river bank whilst on the opposite side of the line the turntable and locomotive yard stand on the site of the erstwhile NER engine shed demolished in the early 1900's. To the right of that turntable is another, smaller, table which marks the position of the ex-MR roundhouse demolished to make way for the New station running lines. The terminal (North) section of City, standing north of the through lines, marks the boundary of the old Wellington, the 1930's concourse forming a right angle to the platforms and leading to the Queen's hotel and City Square. To the south of the concourse is City South and the various extensions of 'New' station can be discerned by the different roof styles employed although the mansard style roof of the original station was used for the south, middle section when that was erected in the late 1870's. At bottom right the main line to the east leaves City on another viaduct up to Marsh Lane. Leeds Central can be made out at the top of the picture and below, between the river and that station stands the power station of the former Leeds Corporation Electric Lighting Co. *P.Sunderland coll.*

LEEDS TERMINI

INTRODUCTION

On May Day 1967, two men and a computer took over the work formerly carried out by seventeen signal boxes controlling the area of Leeds City station and its western approaches. Besides the re-routing of its trains by virtue of new track arrangements, the City of Leeds had at last attained a passenger train service concentrated on one modern station - Leeds City. Not only was the modernised City station convenient for passengers, it rid railway staff of over a century of operational difficulties.

One hundred and fifty years ago, and by virtue of its size, geographical position and comparative speed of growth, Leeds had the potential to be the railway cross-roads of the North of England. However, cut throat politics, short sighted greed and parsimony had been the order of the day, resulting in an unregulated collection of lines and routes that were not necessarily in the longer term interests of the country or even Leeds.

Eventually three major passenger stations served the city, Central, New and Wellington; none of any great architectural challenge and certainly none providing passengers with the full convenience of train changing facilities.

With the present railway network being divided up into competing networks, it is perhaps opportune to reflect on how it took so long for the needs of passengers to be at the forefront of developments at Leeds.

The history of Leeds City, [formerly Leeds New (City South) and Leeds Wellington (City North)] is wrapped up in the arguments, power struggles and personal ambitions of several railway companies and their directors.

In fact, Leeds New would not have come into being if the companies could have agreed on apportionment of land before and during building of Leeds Central in 1850. Instead, the Leeds & Thirsk Railway 'upped sticks' and transferred their services to the temporary Leeds Wellington station on 1st May 1850; the London & North Western Railway followed them five months later when the permanent station opened but only on a small scale as the LNW kept a toe-hold firmly in place at Central whilst that station was being developed. The Great Northern Railway meantime had transferred their trains down from the high level station to a new station on its low level goods site on 14th May.

Although there had been some form of central planning at this crucial stage in the City's development, it was the lack of lasting agreements and continuing squabbles during those early days that was to be the cause of passenger frustration and operational headaches well into the next century.

LEEDS CENTRAL

As already alluded to, the early years of Leeds Central station were far from smooth. An Act of Parliament of 22nd July 1848 ratified an Agreement for joint use of Central station by the following railway companies:- Great Northern, Leeds & Thirsk, Leeds & Dewsbury, and Leeds & Manchester. The GNR arrived in October 1849 and shortly afterwards drew up plans for its own station which it intended to build at low level close to Central. Because it had no direct route of its own yet into Leeds, the GN access to Central meant that its trains had to reverse at Gelderd Junction, a situation it was far from

happy with. Vacating Central in May 1850 for its own low level facility, the GNR was to return to Central in October 1857 when it at last got direct access through its involvement with the Bradford, Wakefield & Leeds Railway. The low level GNR station consisted a single island platform sited between the GNR goods warehouse and the Leeds Northern goods warehouse. The platform was accessible from Wellington Street where the passenger booking office was located.

The situation at Central by 1854 saw the station layout looking like something that would be recognisable a century later. From the concourse (Wellington Street) end, and looking left to right, there was an LNWR platform with its south face butting up to a goods warehouse, next a middle stabling road then another LNWR platform with two faces, then another stabling road and finally an L&YR platform with one long face and a shorter (north) face which formed an island platform. The LNWR facilities were somewhat dominating according to plans of the period. By the station throat, on the south side of the line, the LNW had a three road carriage shed and a four road engine shed accessed via a 42ft turntable.

Once the GNR returned to Central the platforms were shared equally but the LNW realised that it required more space and as the other two companies sharing the facility had no desire to invest in a larger station it was only a matter of time before opportunity, in the shape of the North Eastern Railway, gave them a reason to invest in a more desirable location.

After this period of unease with the railway companies, Central station settled down to the everyday business of serving its passengers with services to London (King's Cross), Manchester and Liverpool via the L&Y, local services to Bradford, Wakefield and towns within the West and North Ridings of Yorkshire. The L&NWR (through the 1848 Joint Station Agreement of the L&DR) kept up its presence there too albeit greatly restricted to one train a day after its 1869 re-allocation to New station.

The ornate ironwork supporting Central's roof give away the station's origins. *Peter Sunderland.*

Time for work. Part of the morning rush-hour at Central in 1955. *D.Beilby coll.*

Central's platforms adequately coped with the booming passenger traffic of the 1880's and 90's. In fact it was never unable to cope with its burden except when the occasional derailment or minor accident blocked some or all of its restricted approaches from the west.

Engine servicing facilities by 1906 consisted a 60ft turntable and a coal stage used by both the GNR and LYR.

The Grouping of 1923 saw the London & North Eastern Railway become the biggest user of Central with the London Midland & Scottish Railway cross-Pennine services of the old L&YR taking a smaller proportion of the traffic. The LNER introduced prestige Pullman trains on its accelerated services to the Capital - *THE HARROGATE PULLMAN* (1923) renamed *THE QUEEN OF SCOTS* in 1927 which reversed at Central on its journeys to and from London to Edinburgh and Glasgow and return. This train, when introduced, ran only as far as Newcastle but was extended to Edinburgh in July 1925 but from September was rerouted via Church Fenton and ran direct to Harrogate, missing out the Leeds stop but from May 1928 it reverted back to the Leeds route. *THE HARROGATE SUNDAY PULLMAN* was introduced in 1927 followed in 1935 by *THE YORKSHIRE PULLMAN*. From 1937 the streamlined *WEST RIDING LIMITED* brought the Gresley A4's into Central. These services were suspended during the war years and all but the latter were re-instated after the conflict to be joined in 1949 by two more prestige trains, though not of the Pullman variety - *THE WEST RIDING* and *THE WHITE ROSE*. The LNER and BR Eastern Region had placed these trains in the hands of their most trusted and powerful locomotives, consequently Central saw (from July 1930) the likes of Gresley's A3 and A4 Pacifics, Peppercorn's A1 Pacifics and, taking over from steam in the early 1960's, the 3,300 h.p. English Electric 'Deltic' diesel locomotives. It is worth remembering the Locomotive Exchange's of 1948 when those engines trialing on the ECML all worked into Central with trains from King's Cross. From the London Midland Region came a 'Duchess' Pacific No.46236 CITY OF BRADFORD and 'Royal Scot'

No.46146 THE RIFLE BRIGADE, the latter type no stranger to Leeds; the Western Region turned out 'King' No.6018 KING HENRY VI whilst the Southern Region candidate was 'Merchant Navy' No.35017 BELGIAN MARINE. In August 1952 a Western Region diesel railcar, W20W, appeared and was apparently taking part in trials to Harrogate and return.

When British Railways came into being, the authorities took a long hard look at the Leeds passenger termini situation and Central came out as the No.1 contender for closure. During the post-war years hardly anything was done to make the place any better or more efficient and only minimum maintenance was carried out to keep it functioning safely. All the various surveys of the period came up with the same points - platforms needed lengthening, the concourse was not big enough, there was bad access from the street, the roof needed renewal (estimated cost £100,000), car parking was bad, staff amenities were non-existent, resignalling was required - total cost approx £1½ million! As regards the roof, it was in such poor condition that the glazing no longer existed by the early 1950's and whenever there was inclement weather there was little shelter for those using the platforms.

It was not all bad for the station during the early 50's. Perhaps it may have been an interim measure but in June 1954, BR introduced diesel multiple unit trains onto certain services from Central. These were in fact the first such trains to be put into regular daily service in the country. The scheme involved the routes to Bradford (Exchange), Harrogate and Knaresborough and within weeks patronage of the new trains had almost doubled compared with the former steam locomotive hauled trains. But 'teething' troubles, which seem to affect anything new, soon brought chaos. The dmu's were withdrawn for rectification and steam locomotives resumed working the local passenger services. However, many of the engines used prior to the introduction of the diesels had been either sent away to other districts or withdrawn which left something of a shortage of motive power. As was the norm in such a 'crisis', locomotives from far and wide were sent to help out with the result that some real 'strangers' were to be seen at Central.

With the 'teething' problems sorted out, the dmu's were soon back in service and, winning new friends. Punctuality and shorter journey times, coupled with cleanliness, all helped to bring back commuters and shoppers to the railway.

By 1958, when some 2.5 million passengers passed through Central, the steady increase in passenger revenue saw a five-fold increase during that year as against the twelve month period prior to the introduction of the new diesel trains. Such was the success of the dmu's that a further batch of units was allocated to the routes radiating from Central. During the interim period other routes were graced with various models of disel multiple unit, all well received by the travelling public and train crews alike.

City station was not without the presence of the d.m.u. either, and from there the new trains were worked on longer routes to places

Gresley A4 Pacific 4495 GOLDEN FLEECE ready to depart Central for a trial run to London King's Cross with the *WEST RIDING LIMITED* on Thursday 23rd September 1937. Resplendent in Garter blue livery with stainless steel numbers and lettering, 4495, along with 4496 GOLDEN SHUTTLE, had been chosen as the engines to work the new streamline service from Leeds. 4495, as GREAT SNIPE and in green livery, was less than two weeks old when it was recalled into Doncaster works on the 11th September 1937 for repainting and renaming. The sudden transformation was required because the designated A4, No.4497 GOLDEN PLOVER, would not be ready in time for the start of the service on the 27th September. With the advent of war such luxuries as this train were curtailed. *Yorkshire Post.*

Central's concourse during the ASLEF Strike of 1955, deserted except for a courting couple and mother with child. Virtually every bit of vertical surface is festooned with adverts for all manner of things - from industrial v-belts to the intelligence of *Daily Mail* readers. Advertising on station concourses was big business at the time and although deemed perhaps to be untidy today, they did brighten up what were otherwise rather drab and austere surroundings. The fares to Bradford note, were 9d (4p) single and 1/3d (6p) return. It cost the same for your dog if you wanted to take it to Bradford. *D.Beilby coll.*

such as Hull and services across the Pennines. By 1961 a dedicated fleet of six-car units, complete with buffet car, were plying between Hull, Leeds (City), Manchester (Exchange) and Liverpool (Lime St.) and certain intermediate stations. The coast-to-coast 'Trans-Pennine' units with further refinements to passenger accommodation, and no less than four of their six cars powered, won over many would-be road users for the next decade.

A service from Central to Manchester (Victoria), over the old L&Y route via Bradford (reversal) and Halifax was another of the success stories of the new diesel scheme. Large numbers of locomotive hauled rolling stock and even the locomotives themselves were made redundant by the steady introduction of the dmu. The writing was 'on the wall' for the steam hauled 'local' and medium distance passenger train.

The writing was on the wall too for Central. Closing its doors on the last day of April 1967, it was demolished during the summer and autumn until, by the end of the year, no trace remained. Hardly one of the great cathedrals of the steam era, the station had, once the 1850s squabbles were swept aside, a long and distinguished history though its presence long outlasted its usefulness.

LEEDS WELLINGTON

Wellington was the Midland Railway terminus in Leeds. Replacing a temporary station (opened 1846), the terminus proper opened in October 1850. Like Central, it was neither grand nor of any great architectural consequence but it was functional and it had a prime position in the centre, its frontage opening out onto City Square.

It was built, in the main, on a series of bridges, some of which spanned the River Aire where that waterway turned southwards from an easterly course through the centre of Leeds. It was approached from the west over a two track main line which spanned the Leeds & Liverpool canal. In 1851 the station layout consised of eight tracks. There were four platforms - General Arrival platform (north side), two stabling roads with connecting turntables, island platform (middle) for arrivals and departures to Bradford, Liverpool, etc., two

stabling roads with connecting turntables, Departure platform (south side) for London, York, Hull, Newcastle, etc. Three roof sections, each of the single pitch type with raised central smoke vents, covered the platforms. To complete the layout a sixteen road roundhouse with an adjacent workshop was sited on the south side of the station layout.

Over the ensuing years the platform layout altered to meet operational conditions and further platforms were brought into use first on the south side in 1872 and later, in 1918, when extensions were made to the north side platforms. A carriage shed occupied land to the south of the station but this was damaged by fire in 1892 and was never replaced though a repair shop was erected alongside the river at the western end of the layout. The tracks of the former carriage shed were kept in situ and this area remained a stabling point for coaching stock until the redevelopment of City station in the 1960's. The locomotive roundhouse was demolished to make way for the approach lines of Leeds New station in 1869; the larger replacement shed being built at Holbeck. However, a turntable remained in use on the site of the former round shed until the early 1960's.

In 1863 the Midland erected a fine hotel, named the Queen's, on land opposite the Wellington frontage. The hotel was extended some four years later and remained until replaced in 1937 by a new building of the same name built on a different site slightly to the west and north of the old Wellington.

With the opening of the Settle-Carlisle line in 1876, the Midland started to run its Anglo-Scottish services through Leeds but the trains had to be reversed at Wellington. At first this seemed to be a useful 'halfway house' for a luncheon stop but competition from the west and east coast companies for the Anglo Scottish passenger traffic made the Midland give up the luncheon stop and accelerate the turnround times at Wellington. They even got round to lengthening the platforms at Armley station to accommodate the expresses, and a shuttle service was planned to run Leeds passengers the short distance over new tracks to be laid from Wortley Junction to Wellington. This scheme, however, never came to fruition and

Wellington in 1933 from the west end of platform 6/7. On the right stands the great bulk of New station which contrasts with the three modest roof pitches forming the train shed of the former Midland terminus but, within two years work was to start on refurbishing Wellington prior to it becoming part of an enlarged City station. Alongside platform 7 an ex-MR Compound, No.1013, heads an express bound for the north. *Stations U.K.*

After its successful North American tour in 1933, LMS 'Royal Scot' 4-6-0 No.6100 ROYAL SCOT (alias 6152) and its train of the same name arrived back at Euston station, in December of that year. Prior to beginning a nation-wide tour of more than thirty British provincial centres, the locomotive and its train were on exhibition for three days at Euston. Here, on 21st January 1934, the 8-coach *ROYAL SCOT* tour train and 6100, complete with the headlight and bell from its overseas jaunt, is seen in platform 6 of Wellington station where a large number of visitors walked through the coaches before inspecting the engine. The two flags adorning the front of the engine were mounted only whilst the exhibition was in progress as they would be otherwise 'out of gauge'. *W.B.Yeadon coll.*

the expresses from London to Scotland continued to perform the reversal at Leeds right up to the end of steam on BR.

Besides the services to London St Pancras, Glasgow St Enoch and Edinburgh Waverley already mentioned, the Midland ran trains from Leeds to the south west of England via Sheffield, Derby, Birmingham and Bristol. Other routes went to Lancaster, for ferries to Ireland, and Morecambe for the seaside. Local services ran to Ilkley and Bradford.

1927 saw the first named train on the former Midland route between London and Scotland - THE THAMES-CLYDE EXPRESS. Engines were changed at Leeds because of the fact that the train had to run into Wellington and then be dragged out (reversed) in the opposite direction to continue its journey. The same year saw a Bradford-Leeds-West of England train named - THE DEVONIAN - which ran to and from Paignton via Birmingham and Bristol. During the early 1950's BR introduced THE CORNISHMAN onto the West of England route from the Midland's but it was extended to Leeds shortly afterwards. In 1957 another named Anglo-Scottish train was introduced onto the Settle-Carlisle route - THE WAVERLEY; this one though was destined for Edinburgh and not Glasgow but the

same engine changing facilities, with a slick six-minute turn-around, had to be provided at Leeds. This particular train had a forerunner also dating from 1927 but bearing a different name - THE THAMES-FORTH EXPRESS - which was curtailed at the outbreak of WW2.

Motive power at Wellington was generally ex-Midland up to the early 1930's when LMS standard types began to come on stream in greater numbers. Holbeck shed supplied the engines and after the 'small' engines of the former Midland Railway had given way to the larger LMS designs, it was possible to see 'Jubilee', 'Patriot' and 'Royal Scot' 4-6-0s handling the main line passenger expresses. Former LNWR 'Claughton' 4-6-0s had been used on expresses during the 1920's and early 30's, so it was possible to see that type working out of both Wellington and New stations alongside each other. In the early 1960's Holbeck shed acquired a batch of ex-LNER A3's to work alongside the 'Royal Scots' on the northern section of the Anglo-Scottish trains but due to their long wheelbase they had to be turned on either the Whitehall (Holbeck) or Copley Hill triangles because Holbeck's own two turntables were not quite long enough.

A circa 1900 view of the locomotive yard at Wellington with what appears to be an '800' class 2-4-0 on the turntable. This was the site, prior to 1869, of the MR 16-stall roundhouse. In the middle background a LNWR 'Precedent' reverses into Leeds New, probably to work a Manchester service. In the background stands the NER 'roundhouse' with the entrance just discernible behind the gas lamp. The authors apologise for the poor quality of this view but such period scenes are somewhat rare. *R.Griffiths coll.*

LEEDS NEW

As far back as the 1850s, a more direct route from the east into a station of their own, in the centre of Leeds had been desired by the York & North Midland. When the North Eastern Railway was formed, that company even went as far as surveying and planning a route that would take their railway from Marsh Lane to a new station to be built in the centre of the town using a viaduct for access for most of the way. It was an ambitious and expensive scheme but Parliamentary Powers were sought.

However, the thought of so much demolition, coupled with the building of a long viaduct through the heart of the commercial centre of Leeds, set the townspeople against the whole project and so in February 1864 the NER, succumbing to public and Parliamentary pressure, withdrew the 'New Station' Bill.

Within days of the withdrawal of the Bill, another scheme was put forward which this time sited the proposed new station on the south side of the Midland's Wellington station, with connections to other company lines at its west end. The route from Marsh Lane, although now planned on a shorter viaduct, would not pass through any part of the commercial centre.

This scheme was virtually accepted at once by the residents of Leeds who, it must be said, had wanted a new station anyway but 'not at any price'.

J.Whitaker, writing in the *North Eastern Express* more than a century later, mutes the idea that the NER had planned the eventual accepted route long before the withdrawal of their first Bill. This idea seems totally plausible when one considers certain of the factors and personalities involved - subterfuge was not unknown amongst railway companies and their agents.

Two Bills were required to get the scheme underway. One for the new station and the other for the new railway from Marsh Lane.

Both received Royal Assent in July 1865, with the 'New' station opening for traffic on 1st April 1869.

All the railway companies serving Leeds had been approached by the North Eastern prior to lodging the Bills but only the London & North Western were interested. Obviously the Midland, who were to become the less than happy next-door-neighbours, did everything in their power to oppose the scheme whereas the Great Northern and the Lancashire & Yorkshire were happy with their situation at Central.

During the four year period of building work of the Leeds New Station, great care was taken so as not to encroach on the adjoining Midland property but part of the old MR Wellington roundhouse was in the path of the station approach lines from the west and the land on which it stood was required by the contractors. An offer to purchase the land was made to the Midland who consented but were slow in negotiation. Much correspondence went backwards and forwards between the Midland and the New Joint Station Committee in 1867. Minutes record the frustration of the Joint Station Committee with the Midland who were dragging their heels completing their new shed at Holbeck. Apparently the Midland at the time were having a few problems themselves and were unable to complete the Holbeck sheds in the time previously stated. However, in May 1868, the MR eventually sold the land and roundhouse to the Joint Committee and work on the new station proceeded without any further hitches.

As if to snub their neighbours, the LNW/NER partnership even built up the viaducts, on which the new station stood, at a slightly higher level than those supporting the Midland's station. When, a century later, the two stations were to form what is now Leeds City, it was found that the difference in levels was to cause more than a few problems to the modern day civil engineers.

It is reported that more than eighteen million bricks and a large amount of cut stone were used in the bridges and viaducts forming the foundation of the station and its approaches. Further enlargement of the station, on its south side, was carried out during the late 1870s and by 1879 Leeds New station had nearly reached the limit of its enlargement which was to suffice until the middle of the 20th century. The extension reportedly cost the two companies a quarter of a million pounds between them.

A new subterranean world of vaulted arches was formed by the foundations of the station and many of these were rented out to small companies. The vaults created a series of continuous tunnels, each about 80 yards long, running beneath New station and linking up with older ones beneath Wellington, all running parallel between the Aire and a north-south running basin of the Leeds & Liverpool canal. Side vaults, running east to west, connected many of the arches forming a huge manmade labyrinth. Over the canal basin itself the railway was supported by a bridge of wrought iron girders on masonry pillars. (This area is nowadays the home for numerous

Nothing changes. Holiday queues at City in the late 1950s. Were you here? *Authors collection.*

craft and gift shops and has the title Granary Wharf.)

Occupying a number of the arches was a soap works and its associated storage area. It was in this storage that a fire, discovered in the early hours of 13th January 1892, caused great damage to the railway above as it burned all day and well into the night. Some 1,600 tons of flammable materials were involved including oil, resin and tallow. During the height of the blaze the local fire brigade called in reinforcements from surrounding towns. Inevitably with such a conflagration, great damage was done and many of the bridge girders collapsed as the incredible heat enveloped them for hours on end. By first light of the 14th, the scale of the damage was clear - no trains could enter or leave New station by the western exit as the bridge and all the tracks running over it had collapsed into the canal below. Even the tracks into Wellington station had been affected though it was possible for the Midland to run trains over the main running tracks with care; only the carriage lines and shed had any appreciable damage.

Luckily, both stations were unaffected structurally but services in and out of New station had to be diverted to Central causing great inconvenience there, but advantage was taken of the forty-odd year old running Rights.

Within ten days of the fire a large temporary bridge, made from timber drawn from merchants along the east coast, had been erected and services at the New station had returned to virtual normality by the 24th January.

Coinciding with the 1879 enlargement, the LNWR built a viaduct which opened for traffic in 1882. The new railway was for their exclusive use and now took their main line westwards, passing to the south of Whitehall Junction, over the Midland at Holbeck and to a point where it met the old main line near Farnley some three quarters of a mile away. The decision to build this new independent line came about because of the congestion and hold-ups at Whitehall Junction where the Midland main line had to be traversed. The LNWR paid a handsome annual rent to use this short stretch of railway between their line and the New station approaches but this did not alter the fact that the Midland could and often did delay the LNW passenger trains. LNWR goods trains continued to use the junction at Whitehall which kept the new line clear for passenger trains.

The LNWR and NER kept themselves very much apart in the station; each had their own platforms and through services between the companies were virtually unknown until the late 1890's when through trains from Liverpool and Manchester were run via Leeds to Newcastle and also to Hull.

Through goods lines were provided on the south side of the 1879 station enlargement and these lines could be used to hold goods traffic until a suitable interval arrived for their continued progress.

Further extensions were carried out in the late 1890's when three sections of transverse roof were erected at the west end of the train shed.

All sorts of LNW and NER locomotives worked the trains to and from New over the succeeding years. After Grouping LMS and LNER 'Standard' types began to infiltrate but the old company engines still 'ruled the roost'. Even in the mid 1930's it was possible to see engines of the following LNER classes: A7, A8, B13, B15, B16, C7, C12, D20, D21, D49, G5, H1, J21, J25, J27, J39, J71, J72, J77, K3, N10, and Q6. LMS engines consisted mainly of post Grouping designs: 'Crab' 2-6-0s, 'Jubilee' and 'Patriot' 4-6-0s, 4F 0-6-0s, the ubiqitous 'Jinty' 0-6-0s, Fowler 2-6-2 and 2-6-4 tanks. The LNWR by this time was represented by very few types except 'Claughton's', 'Princes', and the occasional '19-inch Goods'. From the L&Y were 0-6-0s and 'Dreadnought' 4-6-0s plus tank engines of the 2-4-2 type. Although it was usual for Copley Hill engines to work exclusively from Central, it was not unknown for ex-GN types from that shed to work trains from New. Even railcars, forerunners of the dmu., began to show their faces alongside the tank and tender engines.

LEEDS CITY (NORTH & SOUTH)

After Grouping in 1923, an odd situation arose in Leeds whereby the Chamber of Commerce and Civic Leaders were to point out to the Directors of both the LMS and LNER separately, their frustrations at the state of the termini. These frustrations were well summed up by Mr Bruce, President of the Chamber of Commerce when he stated, "...some of your trains from Lancashire run into one station and some others into another which is nearly half a mile away. The result is confusion." He then pulled no punches by adding, "...the station [Wellington] is utterly unworthy of a great Company [LMSR] like yourselves. It was so in the Midland time; it becomes doubly so under the present amalgamation. It is utterly unworthy of the Town and your great Company. It has the worst station facilities and comforts for passengers of any town with a population over 100,000 in this Country."

When meeting with the LNER Directors a fortnight earlier on 5th June 1925, the response was cool. The Chairman saying that due to the collapse of trade, in 1924, the LMS/LNER had paid over £4,000,000 less than the shareholders were entitled to receive under

the Railways Act. The Civic Leaders assertions about poor train services to Scotland necessitating a change at York was rebutted by, "...one of the best trains in the whole country runs through here, the Leeds-Glasgow."

Work started in 1935 on the physical joining of Leeds New and Wellington stations. Most of the work entailed constructing a new concourse for the Wellington side (City North), which was to link New (City South) station with a new 200-bedroom Queen's Hotel. The bulk of the £750,000 project was actually spent on the hotel with nearly £500,000 accounted for in creating a hotel for Leeds to rival the Midland in Manchester and the Adelphi in Liverpool. The eight floor building was clad in Portland stone and it was the first hotel in the country to be equipped with a regulated ventilation system. As with the building of the station, the foundations have a watery tale - a tunnel (Mill Goit) from the Aire which used to carry water to nearby mills was part filled with concrete and utilised to house the hotel's basement boiler room.

Wellington's new concourse was completed with ticket, booking and parcels offices. An office block, for 400 railway staff, was built alongside whilst beneath a 270 seat cinema was created.

With reconstruction finished and the two stations now joined as one establishment, at least by passenger facilities, the station was renamed Leeds City on 2nd May 1938.

POST WAR DEVELOPMENTS

Following Nationalisation it was realised that a post-war Leeds would be better served by just one main station. Not only would it better serve the travelling public, with all destinations attainable from one point, it would also be operationally more efficient for British Railways.

Leeds Central, with its somewhat hemmed-in position and ancient (compared to City) facilities, was the obvious candidate for closure. It was seen at the time that services could be diverted into

The main concourse at City which arose from the 1930s rebuilding scheme. This 1955 view shows very little public patronage. The building style is typical 1930's with an ornate panelled ceiling fashioned in concrete and supported by huge inverted u-shaped concrete beams. The west wall, as can be seen, contained four huge windows which allowed natural light onto the concourse for most of the day; the low canopies on platforms 1 to 6 making this possible. *D.Beilby coll.*

City without too many operational problems though no specific schemes (except some wartime emergency measures) had been drawn up to implement all the diversions that would be necessary.

City station was in dire need of refurbishment anyway, not just the fabric of the station but also the signalling and routing of trains.

Shortly after Nationalisation, an old established train which worked daily to Glasgow (Queen Street) via York, Newcastle and Edinburgh, was named THE NORTH BRITON. From City it worked eastwards out to York via Church Fenton and was usually A3 hauled.

In 1952 the first steps in attaining the 'one station goal' were taken when plans were drawn up to amalgamate passenger services into one station based on a rebuilt Leeds City station. Powers were eventually obtained in 1959 for the full 'concentration' scheme, although civil engineering work had been carried out previously to prepare some sites for the eventual upheaval. Mr. Arthur Dean (then General Manager of the North Eastern Region) was responsible for overseeing the completion of the massive scheme which, it was planned, would take four years to carry out.

It turned out that some fifteen years would elapse before the 'new' Leeds City station was officially 'opened' by the then Lord Mayor, Alderman J.S.Walsh, on 17th May 1967. Financial restraints during the "You've never had it so good" late 1950s and early 1960s, saw delay after delay, followed by changes, in the many different areas of reconstruction that made up the total scheme.

In July 1963, an amended plan was at last authorised. Reduced in scale from that of the £4.5million, 1959 'scheme', it was also much reduced in capital expenditure. The 'amended' plan was brought about by reviewing the existing railway services in the West Riding and what would be required or still running in the forseeable future (Dr.Beeching was just getting into his stride at the time). Modifications of the whole plan were carried out with costs dominating proceedings. Whittled down to £2.75m, the 'amended' scheme did not include the flyover nor six approach lines at the west end of City station as proposed in the 1959 document. Instead just four approach lines were seen to be required.

The proposed flyover would have been built from a point near to Holbeck High Level station. During its approximate 1,000 ft length, it would have crossed over, then run south eastwards, parallel with the former Midland main line, over Whitehall Road before turning north-eastward towards City station. It would have been used mainly by trains from Bradford and Halifax though trains from Wakefield and London would have had the option of using either the flyover or the ground level alignment over the former LNW/MR junction.

The most expensive parts of the 'concentration' project were undoubtedly the new alignments needed to divert trains, previously terminating in Central, onto lines where they could gain access to City. Three new alignments were built: (1) At Armley Junction from the Harrogate line onto the former Midland main line from the north. (2) Whitehall Curve, alongside the site of Holbeck High Level station, where the former Great Northern lines from the Bradford and Wakefield routes were diverted onto the tracks of the former London & North Western Railway Copley Hill line, just before its junction with the Midland line at Holbeck Low Level. (3) Gelderd Curve, where the ex-GN line from London and Wakefield could gain access via the ex-LNWR Farnley & Wortley viaduct line without traversing the junctions at Holbeck.

As far back as 1943, the LNER had drawn up plans whereby their trains from the Bradford and London routes could be diverted into City station via one of two proposed new lines. The first line, with an easier gradient of 1 in 35, would have connected with the LMS Copley Hill line at a point opposite Copley Hill engine shed. The second, a few hundred yards further east and on a steeper gradient of 1 in 30, would have gained access via the same LMS line opposite Holbeck High Level station. It was this latter 'new line' which was eventually to materialise, slightly modified, as the Whitehall Curve of the 1960s realignment scheme.

One of the first projects of the concentration plan was begun in 1959 when the two bridges spanning the Leeds & Liverpool Canal, at the western end of the City station site, were got ready for replacement by a single bridge giving greater remodelling freedom to any future track layout. The original bridges were built at different levels and the oldest of them, No.11, a wrought iron structure, was some ninety years old and had carried the rails of the former Midland Railway into what was, until 1938, Leeds Wellington station. The other bridge, No.1, dating from a later era, carried four tracks into what had been Leeds New.

The new bridge, which was eventually fully installed by April 1961, consisted a continuous deck of pre-stressed concrete beams, made up into two 60ft spans, the centre pier carried on 2ft diameter concrete piles driven into the canal bed. Allowance was made for barge traffic to continue using the waterway both during and after reconstruction. Once completed, the new bridge allowed the necessary track alterations to be carried out.

Prior to completion of the bridge renewal, its was necessary for engineers to 'take possession' of the tracks running over both bridges at various times though not always together. During the three week period when the former LNW tracks (over bridge No.1) were out of use, it was necessary to lay down a section of track from the the former Midland lines, across the narrow piece of ground that separated them from the lines of Leeds City South. This enabled most trains to negotiate the diversion and gain access to City South whilst others which normally terminated or reversed at City North were handled at stations away from the centre. To list all the affected trains and the permatations of diversions would be too lengthy for this tome.

In May 1961 work was begun on the construction of the multi-storey office block which was to dominate the site of the reconstructed station. Known as City House, the building was on long-term lease to BR after its completion in October 1963. The Taylor Woodrow Group owned the new building, its erection carried out by one of its subsidiaries, Myton Ltd.

To enable work to start on the multi-storey structure it was necessary to demolish part of the station roof and some old offices in the south concourse. The end for the 'old' Leeds City was in sight.

Demolition of the old train shed had started in the summer of 1960 and completion took the better part of four years with sections being dealt with as operational and constructional requirements permitted. Ideally it would have been useful to have closed the station for a couple of months and carried out the demolition job in one go but that was clearly impossible. The station was kept open throughout the seven years of the reconstruction. Admitted, the fact that the station was actually open and in constant use, elongated the construction phase but the lack of funds at critical periods did nothing to hasten the job; nor did the changes and modifications to the original plans, wrought by those restraints, help. The patience of the passengers using the station during the rebuilding was such that BR and the contractors acknowledged them in a pamplet released at the time of the official re-opening in May 1967.

Passenger traffic ceased to use the old Wellington section of City in June 1966 and from the 13th of that month all passenger trains which had previously used City North were transferred to City South platforms. On the 7th November 1966 all passenger services still using Central should have been diverted to City but an objection to the closure of Central was received delaying the inevitable until the following April.

What did those travellers get for their seven year wait? Well, besides more direct routing over the western approaches to Leeds, which was hardly noticed by the great majority of passengers, they got a better station with new, clean amenities; brighter and more accessible platforms and a better more centralised train service.

Two new through platforms were created to complement the three existing through platforms though the total platform face length was reduced from 14,000 to 12,600 ft by a reduction in the number of passenger platforms from 16 to 12. Many of the existing platforms were lengthened, when necessary, to accommodate two trains at once. Care was taken so that any future traffic increases could be accommodated on new platforms constructed in the space left for such purposes. (see Postscript).

The new roof over the platforms covered an area the size of a football pitch and was built to a height that enabled electrification to be carried out (some twenty odd years later) without any major reconstruction.

A passenger subway was created in one of the numerous brick arches below the station; a steel framework provided a new floor level some 15ft above the original floor. Such was the design and cosmetic building work carried out to create the subway that passengers using it are unaware that below them is another larger void. At the eastern end of the new train shed a footbridge was erected for the further convenience of passengers.

Other brick arches below the station were modified to contain an electricity sub-station, central heating and air conditioning plant, signalling and telecommunications control and routing facilities; later on, the renting-out of vacant arches to small businesses saw a semi-subtaranean village created and called Granary Wharf.

On the former City North side, a parcels sorting area was created by building a 5,000 square feet concrete and steel deck over the River Aire; space between platforms once occupied by tracks was filled in and to compensate for that loss of track space, the old Nos.1 and 2 platforms were extended. All the sorting area was covered by a roof and a yard leading onto Aire Street was provided with loading bays for road vans. The vacant space between the parcel sorting area and the north concourse was given over to car parking and enabled more than 100 cars to be accommodated.

A newly created south concourse, with a wide circulating area, was the focal point for shops, refreshment rooms and the ticket office. Above this concourse a five storey office block for BR administration staff and a signalling centre, was built.

During the period of the reconstruction, no less than 88 various contractors were employed to supply and install all the numerous pieces of this vast jigsaw. Although most of the contractors were based in the West Riding, it was still necessary to bring in specialists from as far afield as Essex, Co. Durham and Norfolk. Besides these, there were many different Authorities that had to be consulted and negotiated with such as Leeds Corporation, Ministry of Transport, river and canal authorities and, all the utility companies.

These would have been trying times indeed for the planners and co-ordinators but, add to this the delay caused by financial restraints, then wholesale changes with route diversions and you have one big headache lasting more than ten years. How many of the original personnel 'stuck' with the scheme from start to finish is not known but the fact that it was completed at all is surely a testimony of the determination of all those involved to get the whole thing 'up-and-running'.

On a normal day in the mid-1960s, Leeds City handled some 500 trains. On a summer Saturday this number could attain 550. In the morning (0800 - 0900) and evening (1700 - 1800) peak hours some 80 trains would arrive and depart. In a normal year some 2.75m passenger journeys started from City and the number of parcels handled then exceeded that figure.

Eleven trains ran daily to King's Cross and seven to St. Pancras. Trains to Manchester and Liverpool ran half-hourly for the greater part of the day, alternating between the Bradford and Huddersfield routes.

POSTSCRIPT

During the preparation of this book it was announced that Railtrack, the new owners of Leeds City station, would be creating further running track and passenger platform space in a bid to increase and accommodate extra track capacity at the station. The final layout should hopefully be agreed between Railtrack and the train operating companies by the end of 1998.

This was most welcome news and hopefully will set a trend throughout the country as more motor vehicle owners realise the cost of rush-hour traffic jams, city centre parking and perhaps most importantly, the pollution created by single user motor vehicles.

The railway authorities will have to get things right though. They cannot expect passengers to put up with cancelled or delayed trains. Overcrowding must be eliminated especially on the longer outer suburban or inter-town services and fares must reflect the level of service, comfort and punctuality.

The changes proposed at Leeds will create two more bi-directional tracks at the west end of the station, bringing the total available to six. Two new platforms, numbers 13 and 14 will be created on the south side of the station though a considerable amount of earthworks will be necessary to achieve this.

Costing some £150 million, including signalling, track and building work, the whole scheme will see the station transformed from the 1960s style decor depicted in this book to a new style fit for a city which is apparently the fastest growing city in Europe. The 1930s built North Concourse, which has been empty and neglected for the last thirty years will be transformed at floor level with new shopping and passenger facilities, its former entrance from City Square will once again become the main entrance for the station. Happily the fabric of the North Concourse will be kept as it was built with, of course, new decoration.

Not included in the scheme but planned for the future will be a new train shed over the present platforms 2 to 12 replacing the low roofed and somewhat dismal trainshed built in the 1960s. Its exclusion from the current modernisation project stems from the fact that agreement has not yet been reached as to its final design and the means of funding the work but it is anticipated that it will be a high, lofty structure allowing more natural light onto the platforms below and at the same time give the station a somewhat grand appearance to arriving passengers.

With more than 900 trains a day expected to use the station by the year 2000, Leeds will have a station to be proud of and a transport facility fit for the 21st Century.

(*Opposite, bottom*) **Seen from the Geldard Junction signal box, A3 No.60074 HARVESTER crosses over Gelderd Road bridge after descending the incline from Central with the Glasgow bound QUEEN OF SCOTS in the late 1950's. Once clear of the junction the driver can open up 60074, though by the appearance of the coal piled in the tender it won't be easy for the fireman to maintain steam throughout the journey north.** *P.Sunderland.*

Holbeck High Level in April 1959. The former Great Northern station had closed during the previous July as did its Low Level counterpart directly beneath it on the ex-Midland main line. The view is eastwards looking towards Central which was still thriving although plans were already in place for its demise. *Authors coll.*

Holbeck 6th September 1963. The platforms of the erstwhile High Level station are all that remain by now, likewise on the Low Level. Elsewhere business carries on as normal; at Central the *QUEEN OF SCOTS* awaits departure for the north behind a Gateshead based 'Peak' class diesel-electric whilst on platform 5 one of the new Brush type 4 Co-Co diesel locomotives gets away at the head of a London-bound service. In the Low Level Goods Yard a diesel-mechanical 0-6-0 shunts wagons into the new goods shed. Over on Monk Bridge curve a steam locomotive drifts down to Whitehall with a parcels train and the Up *THAMES-CLYDE* approaches City North behind another 'Peak'. It is interesting to note that all the former Lancashire & Yorkshire Railway owned lines are visible in this view. *Fastline Photographic.*

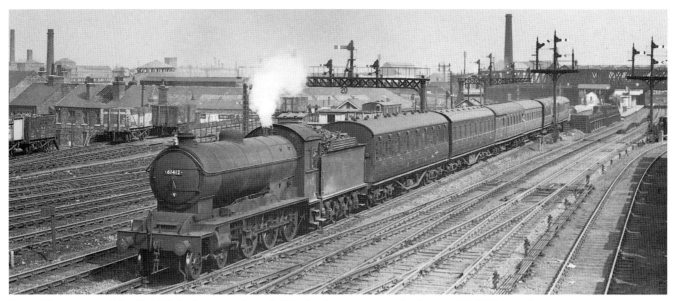

B16/1 No.61412, of Neville Hill shed, passes through Wortley Junction, over the former GN/NER Joint lines, en route to Harrogate with a local train from City in the mid 1950's. Behind the second and third vehicles of the train can be seen the gradient leading up to the high level railway and Central station. Above the locomotive is the curving roof of the former NER locomotive roundhouse which is now in private use and is happily 'listed', one of the very few engine sheds to gain that status. At the time of this photograph Neville Hill engine shed had no less than 33 of these engines allocated, nearly half the class in fact. *P.Sunderland.*

Wortley Junction again in the 1950's with Gresley A3 No.60081 SHOTOVER getting to grips with the northbound *QUEEN OF SCOTS* after its reversal at Central. One of the original A1's, 60081 was rebuilt to A3 in 1928 and had been a Neville Hill engine since 1949. It ended its working days at that shed being withdrawn in October 1962 and was sent to Doncaster for cut-up in May of the following year. To the right of the ex-NER lower quadrant signal is the main line of the former Midland Railway. *P.Sunderland.*

The Central frontage and canopy from Wellington Street in February 1960. Hardly an impressive facade considering the prestige trains the station handled but, plans were afoot, and had been for some time, to close the station and centralise all services onto City station. Due to monetary restraints, Central was to remain operational for another seven years, handling those prestige trains right to the end. Of note in this picture and just visible through the canopy, is the single road locomotive servicing shed built onto the south wall of the train shed. This useful facility was rarely used in latter years though it was handy to stable locomotives there when line occupation made a journey to Copley Hill difficult. The offices facing the yard were occupied by the goods train operations staff on the ground floor and the passenger trains operations staff on the first floor

(opposite) **Platforms 4 and 5 from the concourse, February 1960.** The gloom can be appreciated even though it is midday and the low sun attempts to filter some light through the roof glass. From an operating point of view, the lack of engine release points on these two platforms must have caused some problems when an engine bringing empty stock into either line would be trapped until its train departed. Both platforms 2 and 3 had such a facility for releasing empty stock engines. From this viewpoint it can be seen that platforms 6 and 7, at the top left, were somewhat shorter than platforms 2 to 5. *Fastline Photographic.*

The official entrance to Central station seen from the street in the early 1960s. Even then parking was restricted to 20 minutes and only on Railway business at that. A nice assortment of period motor vehicles occupy the car park; except for the VW Beetle they were, notice, all British built.

Platelayers carry out maintenance on the track inside Central and provide a distraction for passengers awaiting the arrival of their train in platform 3, circa 1955. *D.Beilby coll.*

Mid-afternoon departure time at Central in April 1960. Prominent in this superb scene are, on the left, A3 No.60074 HARVESTER on the Down *QUEEN OF SCOTS* in platform 2, with another A3, No.60039 SANDWICH in platform 5 with the Up *WHITE ROSE*. Alongside 60039, J50 No.68984 goes about its duties as 'station pilot'. In platform 4 an unidentified Stanier Cl.5 heads a short train for Liverpool via the old L&Y Calder Valley route; at Low Moor it would be joined to a similar short train from Bradford. When diesel multiple units eventually took over the Calder Valley services, a reversal at Bradford (Exchange) took away the operational need for the Low Moor stop. The DMU in '6' merits little comment but within a year its larger cousins, the 'Deltics' would have taken over the *WHITE ROSE* services. *Peter Sunderland.*

60074 gets away on time and heads north with its seven Pullman car load. At the rear is the A4 Pacific, which brought the train from London, giving the assemblage a push over the viaduct whence it will drop back and make its way to Copley Hill for servicing. It was a regular occurrence at Central to see locomotives pushing trains out of the terminus. To the right can be seen 'A' box which controlled all the train movements within the station area. *Peter Sunderland.*

(opposite top) Now its the turn of 60039 to get the WHITE ROSE underway on its journey to London. Seen from the landing of 'A' box, the King's Cross based Pacific has little trouble pulling out of the platform. Just above the dome of the A3 a V2 No.60852 can be seen in platform 3. This engine had backed onto its train during the interval between the two main line departures. *Peter Sunderland.*

(opposite bottom) Virtually since its introduction in 1907, the Ivatt N1 0-6-2T had been associated with the West Riding. Although most of the 56 strong class worked at first from King's Cross and Hornsey sheds on the Great Northern suburban services, they gradually began to filter northwards to Yorkshire where they took up residence at Copley Hill, Bradford and Ardsley sheds. By Nationalisation nearly half the class were resident in the West Riding and were ideally suited for working some of the stiff grades and heavy passenger trains in the area. Some of the class had working lives of more than fifty years but all had gone by March 1959. 69447, depicted here at Central in the early 50's was a Bradford engine then and is awaiting departure back to the woollen town. 69447 was withdrawn from service in October 1956, some 46$\frac{1}{2}$ years old. *K.Field.*

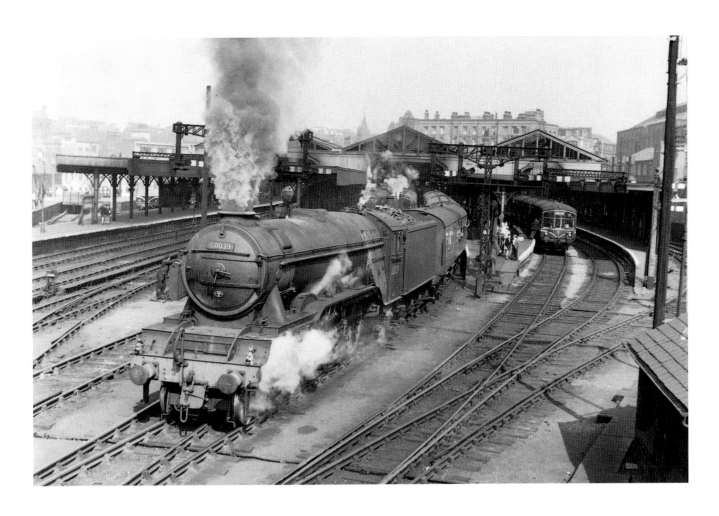

On-your-marks! Was the photographer lucky to catch this line-up of steam power at Central - or was it pre-arranged? Although probably not a unique occurrence at that station, it was nevertheless quite a spectacle to see so many locomotives lined up in such close proximity at the same time. The year was 1955. The locomotives from left were: N1s 69437, 69471; J50 68984; N1 69444 and A1 60123 H.A.IVATT. *E.Blakey.*

(*opposite top*) An unidentified B1 heads a parcels train in platform 1 on a cold day in February 1960. To the left of the engine is another parcels dedicated line with a short bay leading off further to the left. On the far right (platform 5) a King's Cross bound train awaits departure. Notice the smoking open brazier alongside the water column, at the end of platforms 3 and 4; these appliances were necessary during steam days to stop water columns from freezing and, could be found in all sorts of shapes and sizes. Also note the folding boards for sealing off gangway connections on corridor coaches.

(*opposite bottom*) The south side of Central on the same dank February day in 1960. DMU's now have total charge of the local passenger services and early and late style Metro-Cammell units grace the platforms; steam power was still in charge of the main line passenger work but not for much longer. *Authors coll.*

(*below*) Numbered from left to right, all seven platforms of Central can be seen in this February 1960 view from 'A' box. With just a couple of local service d.m.u.s in the station, there is little excitement to lift the gloom of this winter afternoon. *Fastline Photographic.*

With platform No.1, almost hidden on the far right, mainly given over to parcels traffic by the late 1950s, most of the passenger traffic was accommodated in the remaining six platforms. This 24th February 1960 view is looking straight down platform 3 with BR built Mark 1 BCK carriage No.E21044 stabled on the centre road; this particular vehicle had arrived in the morning with the Bradford portion of the *YORKSHIRE PULLMAN*, its function being to provide addition braking capacity for the Pullman cars. The BCK would stable in this position until the evening when it would retrace its steps back to Bradford with the Down Pullman train. Platform 2 is occupied by a 3-car Metro-Camm d.m.u.. The low roof was subject to some major repairs in the mid 1950s but, because of its height, smoke and fumes lingered long after trains had departed, adding to the apparent gloom. *Authors coll.*

Ready to reverse out to Copley Hill shed, 60134 FOXHUNTER, one of that depots stud of Peppercorn A1s, stands at platform 4 after arrival with the Down *WHITE ROSE*. It is April 1960 and steam locomotives still rule the London services. For just over a decade these magnificent locomotives were regular performers on main line trains out of Central; 60134 came to Copley Hill shed brand new in November 1948 and was associated with Leeds for all of its working life. Although it left Copley Hill in April 1962, it only went as far as Ardsley shed from where it was called upon to work from Central. In July 1963 it was transferred back to Leeds but this time to Neville Hill shed where it found employment on services to York and Newcastle until its withdrawal from service in October 1965. *Peter Sunderland.*

A2 No.525 A.H.PEPPERCORN - the last Pacific locomotive built by the LNER and appropriately named after its designer - departs platform 3 with an express for London. No.525 entered traffic on Christmas Eve 1947, initially allocated to Doncaster shed from where it would put in regular appearances at Leeds. Renumbered 60525 in August 1949, it then moved to Aberdeen and was rarely, if ever, seen at Leeds again. This photograph dates from 22nd March 1948.

(centre) Outside Central, three tracks were basically available for all arrivals to and departures from the station. Any mishap could cause havoc with the timetable. Just such a mishap, although not serious, occurred in the early-1950's when this unidentified Pullman car was struck by another train. As can be seen, the damaged Pullman left the tracks and came to rest blocking two of the tracks with the third available if traversed with care. Until the breakdown gang arrive only the one road can be used but once they start to re-rail the Pullman all trains will have to cease until the task is completed. *D.Beilby coll.*

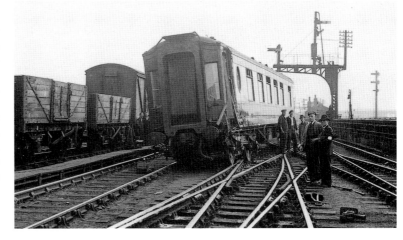

(right) Summer 1955 and this time it's a locomotive 'off the road'. B1 No.61310, from Ardsley shed, is completely 'grounded' but luckily, it is not blocking any platform roads. Because a set of the bogie wheels are on a different side of the track to the rest of the wheels, it will be a bit more difficult to get the engine re-railed but with a lot of shoring up, some jacking and a strong pull from another engine, 61310 should be back on the road in a couple of hours. Damage to the locomotive was minimum but it would be taken back to a shed, probably Copley Hill, and checked over before being allowed back into traffic. *D.Beilby coll.*

23

June 1954 saw the first diesel multiple units working between Leeds (Central) and Bradford (Exchange). This is one of the so-called Derby Lightweight two-car units with interested parties forming a nice group for the photographer on platform 5 in a smoky Central. Shortly after their introduction, these particular units experienced severe problems concerning the torque converters of the final drive. Besides the regular occurrence of total failure, many converters actually caught fire when ascending stiff gradients. Subsequently all new units were delivered with mechanical gearboxes whilst these units soldiered on with modified converters. Having put their problems behind them, the D.M.Us attracted many new travellers to the railway and they were so popular on bank holidays that extra loco-hauled stock had to be used to clear the long queues at Central. *D.Beilby coll.*

(below) The prototype Deltic first visited Leeds in March 1959 when its made two test runs from London hauling a ten-coach train on the 9th and then a 15 coach train two days later. They were certainly earmarked for regular workings to Leeds once the production batch appeared during 1961 and 1962 but none were ever allocated to a Leeds depot. The Deltic's were the mainstay of the London trains from Central right up to closure of the station with Finsbury Park locos covering the London trains and Haymarket examples working in from the north. Finsbury Park based D9003 MELD standing on the centre road between platforms 2 and 3, waits further work on 3rd March 1967. Delivered from English Electric, Vulcan Foundry, during March 1961, D9003 was named MELD at Doncaster Works in July of the same year. Utilised to the utmost by the ECML operating authorities, these locomotives had on average a working life of just twenty years before they were replaced by the Inter-City 125 High Speed Train sets. D9003 was renumbered 55003 in February 1974 and withdrawn in December 1980 just short of its twentieth birthday. Note that a section of the station roof has already been removed pending closure which by now was only weeks away. *Gavin Morrison.*

Central approaches April 1960. J6 No.64277 heads a freight which is en route to Ardsley. The train had started its journey in Wellington Street Low Level yards and in a three directional movement, including being dragged up the incline from Geldard Junction by an unidentified J50 0-6-0T seen at the rear, it has eventually gained the main line for its short journey. Just discernible on the north wall of the viaduct, opposite the J6, is one (no.13) of the Leeds High Level Railway bridge plates. *Peter Sunderland.*

The Harrogate portion of the Sunday Pullman departs Central on the 4th April 1960 behind BR Standard 2-6-4T No.80119. Notice the BR Mk.1. 1st Class carriage unusually sandwiched between the two Pullman cars. *Peter Sunderland.*

Sun and shadow at Central.

It was not intended to reproduce pictures of any of the Leeds goods stations in this book but this picture seemed an appropriate extra because of its Great Northern links with Central and, because of a pre-war document which showed that certain of the Leeds goods stations would play a role in the evacuation of the civilian population of the city. The then secret LNER document, issued in August 1939, listed thirty trains that would, if necessary, depart the Leeds area over a two-day period for destinations in Lincolnshire. The document states that each train would carry 800 civilians at a ratio of ten children to one adult. Nine of the trains were scheduled to depart Central, four from Armley, four from Bramley, three from Beeston and the balance from Hunslet Goods yard. Central Low Level was not listed as an entraining point but could well have been used in the event. This April 1960 view of part of the yard, looking towards Wellington Street, shows much activity with diesel shunter D2243, a J50 0-6-0T and a Fowler 'Crab' going about their business amongst the vast variety of wagons. In the centre background, construction work is underway on a new goods shed which was the site of the temporary GNR passenger terminal before that company took up permanent residence at Central station. Most of this yard was little changed from how it appeared in the late 1840's and in 1960 it must have seemed that things would continue for another century or more but, by the late 1960's traffic patterns and loss of wagon load business to road transport saw the end of this one-time bustling goods facility. *P.Sunderland.*

On Saturday 29th April 1967, Central was closed with very little ceremony except from a large group of enthusiasts (several hundred according to newspaper reports) who had gathered to travel on the last train to depart the station. The honour fell not to a steam locomotive hauled train but instead it was a 4-car diesel multiple unit (strengthened to 8 vehicles for the occasion) which worked the last service, to Harrogate. A special nameboard (HARROGATE FLYER) had been made unofficially for the front of the unit and at 6.15 p.m., precisely five minutes late, the last train departed, watched by the last Station Master Mr A.M.Scott. The last train to King's Cross had departed at 5.50 p.m. This view from Wellington Street, taken later in the summer, shows that no time was wasted getting the demolition teams in to do the necessary. *David Laycock.*

The Up and Down portions of *THE THAMES-CLYDE EXPRESS* were timed to arrive in Leeds at virtually the same time, during the 1950/60 period, and here the Up train departs for St Pancras with a single Stanier Cl.5 at the head (Up train arrival 2.24, depart 2.30; Down train arrival 2.31, depart 2.37). On the other line, Jubilee No.45639 RALEIGH and another unidentified member of the same class wait to back down to collect the Down train from City North. If everything was running to time there would be no problems however, the six minutes allowed to turn the trains around was slick by any means. In the right background, skirting above the rooftops is the 1882 LNWR viaduct. Notice how close the trainspotters are to the main running lines in this April 1960 view. *P.Sunderland.*

Fairburn Cl.4 2-6-4T No.42093 departs City North with a St Pancras - Bradford Forster Sq. slow working in September 1959. The train is passing Canal Junction over the bridges that were to be rebuilt during the next couple of years. *P.Sunderland.*

Sandwiched between the commercial area to its north and the industrial area to the south, the sprawl of Leeds City station is evident in the aerial view from April 1960. The massive rebuilding has yet to start and steam power still rules the main line passenger workings. The 1930's period building, standing on the site of the former Wellington terminal area, stands out against the soot and grime blackened train sheds whilst the Queens hotel stands proudly above it all. The former Wellington side of City was given over to parcels traffic after the rebuilding of 'New' or City South in the mid 1960's but as that traffic was lost to road transport it was left unused except for car parking. The 1935 ticket hall and circulating area was largely vacated and left empty and forlorn but investment and redevelopment in 1998 has brought new life back into the 'forgotten' side of City and passengers will once again use the old platforms 1 to 5 as rail traffic grows once again.

Every route radiating from the Leeds termini can be picked out from this superb aerial photograph taken about midday, 6th September 1963. It reminds one of that song by the Who - *I Can See For Miles*. *Fastline Photographic.*

The western approaches to City and Central stations as viewed from the south in April 1962. The various lines form an interesting if complicated view of the railways in this section of Leeds. Starting at top left, we have the former GNR line from Copley Hill running across the page to right middle. During its virtually straight approach to Central it first skirts the old LNW route from Dewsbury and the west; next it goes through Holbeck High Level station crossing over the ex-MR main line at the same time and then traverses a series of arches where the route from Geldard Junction comes in from the left. Crossing first the Leeds & Liverpool canal, it then parts company with some of the lines from Geldard Junction, which go to Wellington Street Goods Yard opposite 'B' signal box. It then crosses the River Aire, again on a single arch stone bridge; at this point it parts with the lines to the High Level (former L&Y) goods yard. Continuing over the viaduct it passes on its right another goods yard before entering Central passenger station. Notice the new single storey goods shed in the low level yard (seen being built on page 28) is now fully commissioned. The next line to be described again starts at top left, just below the ex-GNR line; this is the old LNWR route created by the Leeds & Dewsbury Railway. As it swept down from Copley Hill the line took a right-hand curve onto the Midland Railway's notorious (for the LNWR anyway) Whitehall Junction which it immediately crossed and traversed left to gain access to the north-eastern segment of the triangle, passed Monk Bridge Iron Works, over a single line of railway connecting that foundry with the MR and up a short incline to Leeds City Junction where the MR line from Engine Shed Junction came in from the right. Within yards of the MR junction, another line joins from the right; the ex-LNWR Viaduct Line dating from 1882, carried on numerous brick arches. As soon as this line is joined, the route crosses the replacement pre-stressed concrete bridge, recently installed, over the Leeds & Liverpool canal. Then, within the environs of City terminus, the line passes, on the right, the former NER locomotive yard with its 60ft turntable. The next line we review also starts at left but this time just below centre. This is the Midland main line from London to Carlisle which at this point curves slightly left approaching Whitehall Junction on its way north. After the junction Holbeck Low Level station is passed , then under the GN line from Central. On the right are the three ex-NER engine sheds (2z\x roundhouses) which became redundant, for locomotive purposes, after Neville Hill shed opened in 1904. On the left is a small goods yard and a gasworks. Skirting the east side of the line now, for a few hundred yards, is the former NER line to Harrogate and the north; as this line diverges right from the alignment of the MR we come to Armley station at the top of the page. Returning to the left side of our page again, we pick out another line just below the MR main line; this is the south segment of the triangle from Engine Shed Junction which comes up from Holbeck to Leeds City Junction. Finally, after passing over Globe Road the line from Whitehall joins from the left whilst the Viaduct Route joins from right. Over the canal bridge the line enters City North, passing the old MR carriage repair shop on the bank of the Aire. *Fastline Photographic.*

(*right*) The afternoon sun of 23rd April 1963 picks out the shiny rail tops at the west end of City station. There appears to be a lull in passenger train movements and a Stanier 8F 2-8-0, hauling a long train of empty coal wagons, takes advantage of this as it heads southwards through Holbeck Junction. At Holbeck shed steam is still very much in evidence whilst the new diesel repair depot, fashioned from the old steam locomotive workshops, can be picked out at top left, by its gleaming roof glass. *Fastline Photographic.*

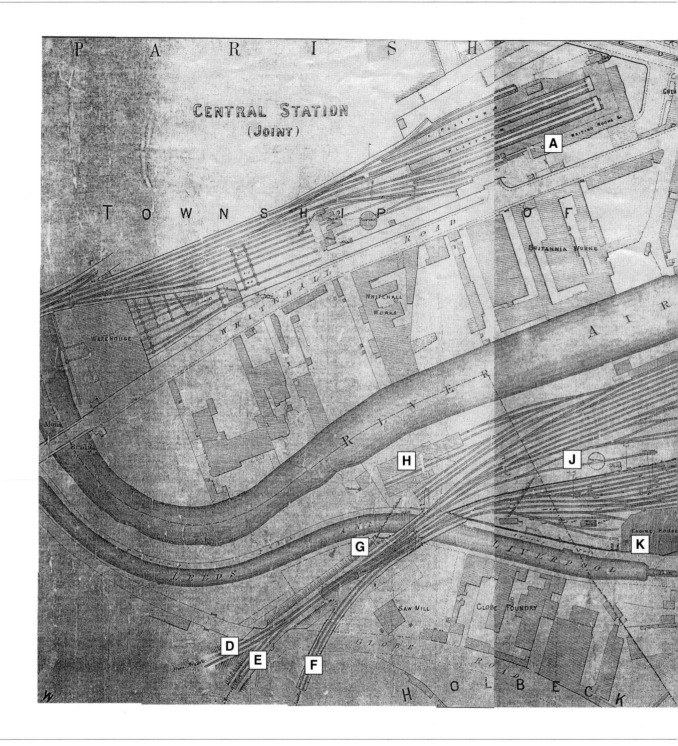

This map dates from the 1890s and is a facsimile of a document of London & North Western Railway/North Eastern Railway Joint origin. The map's prime use was to indicate the lands owned jointly by the two companies at their station in Leeds. Also shown are those areas where the Joint partners had mutual use with the Midland Railway and, those areas where land had been given up by mutual consent in exchange for further land given up by the Midland Company.

The map is also useful as it shows the position of Central station in relation to Wellington Street and New stations. One can appreciate the changes brought about during the 1930s when the London Midland & Scottish Railway, in conjunction with the London & North Eastern Railway, rebuilt Wellington Street

station, the Queens hotel and altered the area bounded by Wellington Street, Bishopgate Street and Mill Goit. Cloth Hall (I) was another building that had disappeared in the 1930s so as to make way for Queen's Square which eventually fronted the new Queen's Hotel. Mill Goit was of course built over as part of the road realignment in that area.

From left to right the points of interest are Central station (A), which was to change very little up to the time of it's closure except for the addition of a seventh platform on the Whitehall Road side. Likewise the Great Northern Hotel (B) was to remain unaltered.

The three routes from the west into Wellington/New were from Bradford (D), Normanton (E) and Manchester (F). The map

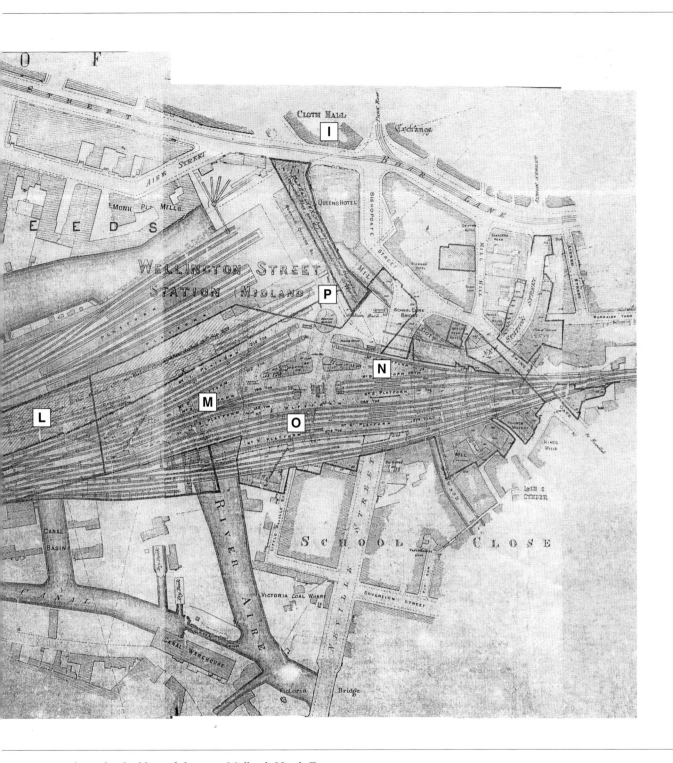

predates the doubling of the joint Midland, North Eastern route (D) from a point at Whitehall Junction to the north bank of the Leeds & Liverpool Canal at (G). The two road Midland Railway carriage repair shed (H) was another building which survived to the end of steam on BR. A little further eastwards and we come to the turntable of the Midland's erstwhile circular engine shed (J), demolished to make way for the running lines of New station. Just to the south of that is the NER locomotive yard with its multi-sided stabling shed (K) containing a turntable and eight radiating roads of varying length, basically a third of the usual accommodation of one of the NER's more conventional square roundhouses.

Next is the Midland carriage shed (L) which suffered during the

1892 fire. Wellington Street station had five passenger platforms and a single parcels platform on its north side on the bank of the Aire. Leeds New consisted ten platforms; numbers 1 to 4 (M) being the terminal platforms for the exclusive use of the LNWR; 8 to 10 (N) were the terminal platforms of the NER whilst 5 to 7 were the through platforms used jointly. Access to the island platform 6 and 7 was then via a subway (O); the footbridge which figures in a number of the later views of the station was added at an unknown date.

Notice the virtually circular ticket booking office (P) sited at the station's pedestrian entrance. This single unit was superseded by two separate booking offices - LMS and LNER - probably shortly after Grouping (see page 36).

On the left is the former North Eastern Railway Locomotive Yard, at the west end of Leeds New, bereft of any motive power on the 11th November 1936. The NER created locomotive facilities on this site in 1871 when they erected a shed to house eight engines. Having something of a leaning towards 'roundhouses', it was inevitable that the company erect such a building on this site but, such were the restrictions of space, only a segment of a roundhouse could be built. Basically it consisted a turntable with eight stalls rather than the more usual, for the period, 24 stalls. The map on page 32 shows the awkward shape of the shed. By 1906 the shed had outlived its use and was demolished; the opening of Neville Hill shed in 1904 gave the NER all the stabling room it needed at Leeds but the yard at New station was still required as a locomotive turnaround and servicing area. A 60ft turntable, which lasted in use until the late 1950s, was installed shortly after the shed had gone. This midweek view was taken to show the recent installation of colour-light signals at New station prior to their being brought into operation. Notice they are sited alongside the existing mixture of North Eastern and LMS semaphore signals so as not to confuse footplate crew, although that said, there was very little alteration to the trackwork on this side of what was to become Leeds City South station. *Authors coll.*

The year 1935 marked King George V's Silver Jubilee. To celebrate the occasion the LMS named all the locomotives of the then unnamed taper-boilered 5XP class. They became the 'Jubilee' class and each one was suitably adorned with a Patriotic or Imperial name. The class leader 5552 swapped identities with the newer 5642 and the latter engine, suitably presented in black livery with raised chrome numbers and chrome finish, then became 5552 SILVER JUBILEE. Typically, for the period, the engine was sent around the LMS system to show off its adornments during the period of Patriotic fervour and, just like the year before when the ROYAL SCOT visited Leeds, 5552 did the same even using the same platform on Wellington station. *D.Beilby coll.*

By the 19th April of the following year, the semaphores are gone and the new signals control the through lines of Leeds City. The LNER loco yard has a couple of customers, ex-NER 4-4-0s of D17 class, in this early morning view. On the extreme right can be seen the 50ft turntable of the former Midland Railway Loco Yard with a Midland built 4-4-0 Compound in close attendance. Like the previous picture, this view was captured on film from the then new signal box Leeds New West, erected in conjunction with the new signalling scheme. Both this and the view opposite show the gloom pervading at the time due to the air pollution of the era. *Authors coll.*

Platforms 3 and 4 at the rebuilt Leeds City North (formerly Wellington) in 1938. Notice the dozens of LEEDS nameplates hanging from the canopy, leaving arriving passengers in no doubt about where they were. The canopy has been finished in the style of the new main concourse although the amount of girder framework in view suggests that other schemes were yet to be finalised. A Bradford train stands at platform 4 with an ex-LNWR 6-wheel van at the rear. Signal Inspector Harry Greenwood, with briefcase and umbrella, strides down the platform to catch his train. *D.Beilby coll.*

Leeds City South circulating area in May 1939, looking out onto the station yard. To the left is the LMS booking office with its LNER counterpart on the right. Considering that so much money had recently been spent rebuilding the old Wellington Street section of the now enlarged station, very little, if any, appears to have been spent on even cleaning this section of the station. Still, if local people wanted to get away from it all for a short time, the East and West coasts beckoned. *Authors coll.*

The concourse of City North looking towards City South in March 1956. Besides the car batteries, perfumed soap, and insurance adverts, some of the other advertising is quite interesting; N.O.M. manure made from wool waste - for progressive gardeners. The shortage of horse manure at the time, no doubt another unrealised victim of the motor vehicle, prompted one enterprising Morley woollen mill to offer its processed waste to horticulturists. W.H.Smith, now no longer vending to railway passengers in Leeds, had a bookstall between the waiting room and enquiry office. On the right are the entrances to platforms 1 to 6; platforms 7 to 16 were accessed through an opening in the end wall below the Yardley advert. During the alterations of the 1960's a new platform (No.17) was created on the outside of the south wall of the station and the sign above the access was duly changed, in the same style, to platforms 7 to 17. The platform did not last too long as No.17 though because the remodelled station required only twelve platforms and 17 was changed to 12 by the time of the official re-opening in May 1967. After that, this wonderful piece of 1930's architecture was unused except as access from Wellington Street and the newly created car park covering part of the old platforms 1 to 6. *Fastline.*

(right) **Girl Guides** crowd the end of platform 12 and grace the B16 locomotive which is about to depart for what appears to be a special working. The headboard is adorned with the Guide badge and the initials B.P. - Baden Powell - 1857-1957. Lord Baden Powell founded the Scout movement in 1908 and the Girl Guides in 1910. Born in 1857, he died in 1941. *D.Beilby coll.*

(left, opposite) **The view** east along platforms 12 and 13 during the rail strike of 1955 The magnificence of the 'New Station' roof and supporting columns show up well in this smoke and traffic free scene. *British Railways.*

37

City Square in March 1958 with the Queens hotel dominating the picture. The Portland stone frontage has not stood up too well to twenty years of grime and pollution. When the hotel was built, the exit road from the station was specially laid with rubber setts where it ran under the building at its east end; thus ensuring an undisturbed sleep for residents with room above the road. At the time of the photograph, trams were still running in Leeds (just about) but, though the tracks are still in place, the trams did not traverse this square any more. For those unfamiliar with the city, the statue of the mounted rider represents the Black Prince. The rounded stone and pillar clad building on the corner of Bishopgate and Boar Lane is the Midland bank, complete with a domed roof; nowadays the building is a cafe. City Square used to be an important tram terminus and had a terminal spur in the centre, the line of which is highlighted by the new paving. *Fastline Photographic.*

(left) Platform 5, City North circa1960. This portion of the station was originally the old Wellington, up to the 1930s rebuilding. In the background is the Queens Hotel. The girder framework built over platforms 3 and 4 during the 1930s has now been utilised for train crew offices and a canteen, though the timber clad buildings have a temporary air about them more reminiscent of a building site office.

(right) Dramatic midday lighting at City South in 1951. The view is westward along island platform 12/13 as seen from the footbridge. *D.Beilby coll.*

(far right) A period view of the City car park shortly before the demolition men arrived. *D.Beilby coll.*

Platforms 11 and 12 of City South in April 1959, just prior to the massive changes of the next decade. The opening in the south wall, where the roof is supported by two cast-iron pillars, depicts the line of Neville Street where it passes under the station. A brick screen was deemed to be too heavy for the supporting girder and the opening was left to conserve on weight. *Fastline.*

(left) One of the older, and some say grimiest, areas of Leeds 'New' in the 1950s. The view is towards platform 16, the terminal platform at the east end of the station. Although much work was carried out on the old Wellington station during the 1930's, this area of 'New' was left untouched. *Authors coll.*

(opposite, top) **B1 No.61038 BLACKTAIL** was a Neville Hill engine from May 1957 until January 1961 when it departed for Gateshead. Prior to it being shedded in Leeds it was a York engine so would have been a regular visitor to the city. On a fine morning in the mid-50's it arrives at City with an express from the east. *E.E.Smith.*

(opposite, bottom) Taking the Slow line past Canal Junction, the Down *THAMES-CLYDE EXPRESS* departs City North behind 'Jubilee' No.45562 ALBERTA. It was usual that 'Jubilee's' worked these expresses south of Leeds and the 'Royal Scot' 4-6-0s took the northbound legs but shortages of motive power meant that such arrangements could be altered to suit the situation as here. *P.Sunderland.*

(centre left) City South 1960, with a luggage trolley from the 19th century and by contrast a brand new Trans-Pennine diesel unit. Such was the railway of the 1960s - old and new thrust together - no wonder that change and modernisation was needed. *D.Beilby coll.*

(below) A general view of Leeds City South in April 1960. It is early afternoon and departures are taking place (or are about to) from most platforms with a Cl.5 and a 'Jubilee' just getting underway with the 1.05 p.m. to Liverpool (Lime St), ex-Newcastle. Steam locomotives still rule the roost. *P.Sunderland.*

(left) Ivatt Cl.4 2-6-0 No.43052, of Neville Hill shed, backs through the east end of the station in February 1959 whilst the harsh winter sunshine creates some marvellous images in this midday scene. In January of the following year a locomotive of the same class, No.43045, working a service from Heysham Harbour, overran the bufferstops on platform 3 of City North. Luckily there were no serious injuries. *P.Sunderland.*

(below) A3 No.60081 SHOTOVER enters platform 11 from the east with the midday arrival from Newcastle in February 1959. The train would continue on to Liverpool via Manchester but behind former LMS motive power. Once detached, 60081 would reverse through the station and on up to Neville Hill shed, which had been its home since February 1949 and would be its last before being withdrawn in October 1962. On the extreme right of the picture can be seen one of the pair of goods avoiding lines which fanned out into four alongside the south wall of the station. *P.Sunderland.*

April 1960 and Gresley A3 No.60036 COLOMBO of Neville Hill shed has just arrived from Newcastle with an express for Liverpool (Lime Street). The A3 is being detached and would later back up to Neville Hill shed for servicing. Its place would then be taken by double-headed engines from Farnley Junction shed for the run over the Pennines into Lancashire via the Standedge route. *P.Sunderland.*

Stanier Cl.5 No.44840 and rebuilt 'Patriot' No.45525 COLWYN BAY have backed down onto the Liverpool-bound express and are ready for the 1.05 p.m. departure. It was usual for the Leeds-Liverpool stage of the train's journey to be double-headed with combinations such as this, with 'Jubilee' and 'Royal Scot' types also employed. In the bay platform a grimy 'Jubilee', No.45655 KEITH, heads a semi-fast bound for Manchester. *P.Sunderland.*

At the east end of City in April 1960, B1 No.61035 PRONGHORN departs for Hull with an express brought from Liverpool by Jubilee No.45708 RESOLUTION. The coaches are a mixture of BR and LNER stock. One of the fascinating aspects of Leeds City was the continual engine changing on inter-regional trains - former LNER route trains were powered by locomotives from Neville Hill shed whilst those going west over the old LNWR routes were powered by engines from Farnley Junction shed. Holbeck engines meanwhile took care of trains both south and north over the old Midland road. *P.Sunderland.*

Another east end departure in April 1960, this time from bay platform No.16, is formed of more modern power in the shape of a Metro-Cammell DMU working a service to Selby. Notice the timber decking of the platform, its starting point marking the boundary where the station runs above the thoroughfare known as Swinegate. Also note the lightweight wall screening used in preference to bricks for the continuance of the north wall over the bridge. *P.Sunderland.*

(above) **Morning departure Leeds City.** A3 No.60086 GAINSBOROUGH is ready to start its journey from the east end of platform 11 with *THE NORTH BRITON*, yet another Leeds to Glasgow service. There is something about this photograph which conveys the romance of travelling long distance by train. This particular train offered inexpensive meals for its passengers in the buffet car whilst a full Table d'hôte was available in the restaurant car. *N.Stead coll.*

(right) Having stated above about the romance of long distance rail travel, the general public were sometimes left high and dry by industrial action. The Special Announcements board proclaims the situation at the end of the rail strike of 1955. Notice the immaculate hand written list of departures. *D.Beilby coll.*

(above) Seen leaving platform 6 in April 1948, with a southbound Midland line service, is newly arrived, Crewe built, Caprotti Class 5 No.44754. A derivative of the LMS Stanier Class 5, the Caprotti equipped engines were introduced with other refinements beside the valve gear and cost, in 1948, more than twice the £6,100 each of the original 1934/35 batch numbered 5000-5069. Initially Holbeck shed received five of these Caprotti locomotives from Crewe: 44753-44757, the latter three, arriving later in the year, also having double chimneys and electric lighting. *D.Beilby coll.*

(left) The cold of January 1955 is emphasised by the steam escaping from 'Jubilee' No.45564 NEW SOUTH WALES as it backs onto the Up *THAMES-CLYDE*. The Down train stands on platform 5 awaiting its motive power for the journey north. Keeping alive its links with the past, the signal box was named Leeds City Wellington. *P.Sunderland.*

One of Holbeck's 'Jubilee's', 45659 DRAKE departs City North with the Up *THAMES-CLYDE EXPRESS* in September 1959. It was usual that 'Jubilee's' handled the southbound workings of this train from Leeds and 'Royal Scot's' took care of the more difficult northbound workings. In the left background stands the Leeds Corporation power station on Aire Street. *P.Sunderland.*

Bradford Manningham shed was responsible for supplying the motive power for the Leeds to Skipton passenger services for many years. The trains travelled either via Ilkley or Keighley and, in 1956, this afternoon train was one that would traverse the Ilkey route headed by former L&Y 2P 2-4-2 tank No.50636 which is being got ready for departure from platform 10. The Lanky tanks were regular performers on the Skipton trains from the mid 1930s and by the early 1950s no less than eleven of the class were allocated to Manningham for such duties though most of these were actually sub-shedded at Ilkley. *K.Field.*

'Britannia' Pacific No.70054 DORNOCH FIRTH alongside platform 5 with the Down *WAVERLEY* in February 1959. 70054 was one of three Britannia's allocated to Holbeck from October 1958 until September 1962 for working the northern section of the Anglo-Scottish expresses. *P.Sunderland*.

Carnforth 'Jubilee' 45686 ST. VINCENT prepares to depart platform 4 with the 1.55 p.m. service to Morecambe. The bulk of the Queen's hotel dominates the skyline whilst to the left is the office BR office block situated on Aire Street. *P.Sunderland*.

In September 1959 a Newton Heath Stanier Cl.5 No.45225 comes off Canal Junction and onto the former LNWR 'Viaduct Line' with a semi-fast for Manchester (Exchange). *P.Sunderland.*

45225 gathers pace as its crosses Globe Road and heads westward over the 1882 viaduct. *P.Sunderland.*

A group of dramatic pictures showing the accident involving a 138-ton diesel locomotive and an 8-car diesel multiple unit on the eastern approaches to City, 10th August 1961. The diesel locomotive, running light to Neville Hill shed, overran signals and collided with the Leeds-Scarborough DMU resulting in one passenger fatality and two injuries. Leaking fuel oil caught fire and the leading car of the d.m.u. sustained some damage. As can be appreciated, the south wall of the viaduct was demolished and several motor vehicles in a yard below were crushed by the falling masonry but the casualty figures could have been much higher if the affected carriages had fallen into the street. Crowds in The Calls appear to be awaiting further developments - perhaps the arrival of the breakdown gangs who would, it appears, have a somewhat dangerous and precarious situation to sort out. Severe operational problems resulted from this accident as all traffic to and from the east would have had to have been diverted by another route and Neville Hill shed would have been cut off. For those interested, the 'Peak' was D103 and the two overturned vehicles of the passenger train were E51440 and E59533, both survived to and after repair were returned to traffic. At the subsequent inquiry, the Inspecting Officer, Col. D. McMullen concluded that the signal which was overrun was badly positioned (three similar though less dramatic incidents had occured in the previous two years) and that was repositioned shortly after this accident. *D.Beilby coll.*

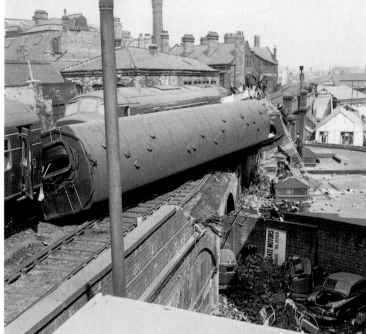

(*above*) Looking east from Canal Junction signal box in May 1960 after the first of the new bridges was installed on the north side of the junction. The bow-girder bridge remaining on the south side of the junction dated from 1869 and was to be replaced during April and May 1961, necessitating closure of the two former LNWR tracks crossing the bridge. During closure a temporary track was laid through the old Wellington locomotive yard to connect the City South lines with those of City North thereby allowing through running of certain trains such as the Liverpool - Newcastle expresses although a full timetable could not be maintained for all trains normally using the route into City from the west. *D.Beilby coll.*

(*right*) Mid-April 1961 and one of the Motive Power Department breakdown cranes lends a hand with dismantling the 1869 bridge. A number of cranes from various depots, even one from Darlington, were used at different stages during the three week period of bridge reconstruction. *D.Beilby coll.*

The north girder of the North (Wellington side) Canal bridge was removed from the site on Sunday 10th April 1960 by BR Standard 9F No.92045 with an unidentified WD Austerity 2-8-0 following in close attendance. The girder weighed some 130 tons and although it was not a problem haulage wise, for the 9F, it was as can be seen somewhat 'out-of-gauge'. Great care was exercised throughout the journey to Holbeck High Level where it was to be stabled, pending further arrangements, and several shunting moves were required just to get the load across Whitehall Junction. Here the train has just halted on the junction after negotiating Monk Bridge curve and is awaiting a clear road prior to its next movement. *P.Sunderland.*

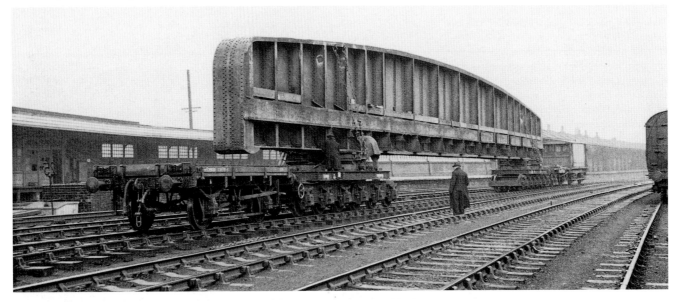

The huge girder is dumped in the sidings alongside Holbeck High Level station. The engineers check the lashings and mountings so that all would be safe during the period of storage. When it eventually left this siding is not known but for further evidence of its long residence at Holbeck, and of its south side counterpart grounded at Holbeck Junction, see the aerial view of Holbeck taken in September 1963 on page 58. *P.Sunderland.*

The first section of roof to be taken down was the transverse section at the western end of the station; the last part of Leeds New added by the joint partnership of the LNWR and NER. During the early days of demolition, in October 1960, mobile road cranes were brought onto the site by special train to lift the lattice girder roof supports from their cast-iron columns. This is Sunday 2nd October when this area of the station was closed off to all normal rail traffic. In a bid to keep the station working as normally as possible all these heavy and precarious lifting jobs were carried out on Sundays. *Fastline Photographic.*

The roadway called New Station Street where it passed over Neville Street. This was the main vehicular approach to City and in this June 1961 view the canopy cladding has just been taken down in preparation for starting work on the new office block 'City House'. *Fastline Photographic.*

(left) Manchester based demolition contractors Connell & Finnigan take apart the train shed of City South whilst in the background the new office block dominates the scene in 1963. The coats-of-arms of both the L&NWR and the NER adorn the cast iron fillets of the roof supports. An interested observer of the demolition team's tactics was lucky enough to acquire one of the fillets, complete with coat-of-arms.

(below) Looking eastwards along platforms 12 and 13 in June 1963 from the old footbridge. The 12-storey office block is nearing completion but work on the station appears to have ground to a halt. The different roof styles show the limits of the original 1869 mansard station roof on the left whilst the later 1879 extension is represented by the single pitch roof covering the east end of the platforms. By September all these roofs had been torn down leaving the platforms open to the elements for winter.

Chaos 6th June 1963. This is the frame of the mansard roof covering the terminal roads of the former LNWR section of 'New' station (platforms 7 and 8 of City). Trains are still using platform 8 but passengers were well aware of the dangers lurking all around them. *Fastline Photographic.*

From the same vantage point just a month and ten days later, the difference is obvious. Trains are now using platform 7 also, and a bookstall (was this Menzies?) has sprung up and is trading amidst the chaos and corrugated iron shelters. Note the centre advert, for a train exhibition, on the large hoarding above the entrance to the 1930s concourse; it proclaims that it was the Leeds June Dairy Festival to be held 4th to 6th July! *Fastline Photographic.*

(*above*) A view from the ramp of the old cast-iron footbridge, looking east. City is in the throes of rebuilding and temporary platforms are being created to allow building work to proceed without too much disruption to traffic. Notice the new platform 17 built along the outside of the south wall of the original train shed. A BR Sulzer Bo-Bo diesel stands on the middle road between the old platforms 11 and 12. *D. Beilby coll.*

(*right*) September 1963. Three and a half years on from the photograph on page 30, and a dramatic change has occurred. Gone are the train sheds erected jointly by the LNWR and NER. The new City House office block has sprung up and is nearly completed. Passengers will have noticed during this period just how cold and windy those open platforms were without a cover. Steam locomotives are still much in evidence but so too are main line diesel locomotives and, the ubiquitous diesel multiple units. Also gone is the North side locomotive servicing area turntable, whilst that on the south side is still in situ and performing a function. *Fastline Photographic.*

(*above*) Holbeck and the western approaches to Leeds termini as seen from the north in September 1963. This view demonstrates the dominating nature of suface transport in the Holbeck area of Leeds, with the railways occupying the lion's share of space. Prominent in the middle foreground are the two and a half 'true' roundhouses of the former North Eastern Railway. Although vacated by the Locomotive Department of the NER as long ago as 1904, in favour of the new depot at Neville Hill, the buildings were still performing a useful function for private industry. The largest roundhouse, at the bottom of the picture was happily given 'listed building' status and today (1998) is enjoying a refurbishment. The number of railway goods yards is proof of a once massive industry when most of the country's goods was carried by the railway companies; even at this late date in the age of steam there are numerous goods wagons gracing the myriad of tracks. But, radical changes were afoot in 1963 and by the end of the decade much of the railway infrastructure had gone. The high level line from Holbeck to Central station and its associated goods yards would soon be a memory as a reminder. Remember the girder removed from the north side of the canal bridge on the approaches to City and taken to Holbeck High Level for temporary storage? The eagle-eyed amongst you will have spotted it grounded alongside the original former LNWR main line, near Whitehall Road goods, where it leaves Whitehall Junction and heads westwards. How long the girder remained there, before it was eventually cut-up, is unknown to the author. *Fastline Photographic.*

This August 1963 view, from the near-completed office block, shows the western approaches to City with the new parcels bridge taking shape. Trains continued to use the station throughout the reconstruction phase though completion of the whole project was still nearly four years away. Note the clerestory roofed coach in the Wellington carriage yard, towards the western end of platform 7; I wonder what happened to that? Amongst the by now ubiquitous DMU's steam power is still in evidence with a 'Jubilee' awaiting departure from platform 12, and a couple of 2-6-4 tank engines sorting out coaching stock in various areas of the station. On platform 5 a solitary 'Peak' heads an Anglo-Scottish express. *Fastline Photographic.*

(above) This April 1964 view from the new multi-storey office block (City House) shows off nicely the work done during the 1930's modernisation of Wellington. The architecture of the period stands out against buildings from earlier and later periods. The long, narrow roof of the concourse runs at right angles to the platforms whilst the bulk of the Queen's can be appreciated. A temporary corrugated iron roof gives some shelter to intending passengers as they arrive at City by motor vehicle whilst pedestrians from City Square can take advantage of the pavement canopy hanging from the 1930's building housing the booking office. The building in the immediate foreground is of interest also, with its ground floor facing Swinegate and its rear/side aspect facing onto the station approach road at second floor level. This structure was deemed not to survive the rebuilding of City, the space it occupied being required for car parking. *Fastline.*

(left) In 1958 the floor of the North Concorse was treated to a wash and scrub by a firm of outside specialists cleaning contractors. With twenty years of grime covering the original tiled floor it appeared to be more like a tarmac roadway than a passenger circulating area. With the aid of mechanical scrubbing machines and good old 'elbow grease', the first section of tiles is 'uncovered' and looking more like an internal floor. *Authors coll.*

By October 1963, the overall roof of the new trainshed was being erected and this view taken on the 24th of that month shows the contractor's road crane 'hogging' the pavement of platform 10/11. All the roofing materials were brought into the station by rail and the crane itself was probably positioned this way. Mail and parcels can be seen along the length of the platform and no doubt passengers were still boarding trains on '11' whilst construction was proceeding around them. *Authors coll.*

The scale model of the new Leeds City Station presented to the public before the commencement of rebuilding. The station was finally completed as depicted except for the overall roof of the Parcels Depot which on the model has no form other than a flat featureless surface; perhaps this indicates that this area of the building was still to decided upon. The North Concourse, though included on the model. had no foreseeable future in the 1960s, other than as a public thoroughfare, and it was not demolished at the time. Now some thirty years after it was all but abandoned it is to be reborn and incorporated into the refurbished Leeds City. *D.Beilby coll.*

November. Much to everyone's relief, the new roof has started to take shape but passengers and staff are still threading their way through the building site that is City South. *Fastline Photographic*.

The Wellington side of City in September 1966. Evidence of recent track relaying and realignment can be seen with new ballast having the appearance of newly fallen snow. Steam motive power is still evident but passenger trains in this section of City were soon to be a thing of the past as the platforms were given over to parcels traffic and all passenger services diverted to City South. *Fastline Photographic.*

During the rebuilding of the 1960's, many of the voids below City station were required for housing electrical apparatus for signalling, ventilation and heating. This July 1969 view shows some of the original 1870's stonework on the left, and facing is some of the new brickwork screening much of the equipment associated with the new station. Although on-street parking was not then such a problem as today, many people used the arches as a convenient parking area. One of that decades most popular motor vehicles, the Ford Anglia, is well in evidence amongst its contemporary ilk. *Authors coll.*

Almost complete. This was the view of the station in April 1967, just days before the official opening of the new facilities. A couple of ballast trains are stabled on the old Wellington site and diesel locomotives now outnumber the few steam locomotives still shunting the parcels traffic. *David Laycock.*

The final word belongs to an era which is now but a memory. Hopefully this album of views has reawakened some of those memories, not only for the natives of Leeds but also those of us who travelled to Leeds to sample its delights; also the authors hope that it gives an insight into what was happening on the railway scene at Leeds during a period of railway history which was never less than chaotic and was always interesting.

Halcyon days at City North, April 1960. Trainspotters throng the end of platform 6 to await the arrival of the Up and Down *THAMES-CLYDE* and in the same platform road a Stanier Cl.5, complete with headboard waits to attach itself to the Up train. On the right there is much activity in the carriage sidings with Ivatt LMS designed locomotives collecting or depositing passenger and parcels stock. *P.Sunderland.*